# freedom in FORGIVENESS

## MIKE NOVOTNY
with bonus Bible study by Ben Sadler

Published by Straight Talk Books
P.O. Box 301, Milwaukee, WI 53201
800.661.3311 • timeofgrace.org

Printed in the United States of America
ISBN: 978-1-949488-59-3

# contents

# *introduction*

This book is about forgiveness. And that's why my colleague Pastor Jim emailed me. Pastor Jim is famous for his heart. On the StrengthsFinder personality test, my dead-last strength, empathy, is Pastor Jim's number-one strength. So when I started to prepare for this book, my mind went immediately to passages—all the Bible passages that use the words *forgive, forgave, forgiven, forgiveness*. There are 128 of them, by the way. But while I was thinking of the passages, Jim was thinking of the people. He was thinking of you. And he reminded me that whenever the word *forgive* is mentioned, people start to think of the most painful parts of their past.

In other words, he reminded me of something like this. Think of a pile of stones. Can you imagine it? The stones in this pile are like the sins that people have committed against you. You were neighbors who waved hands or coworkers who shook hands or spouses who held hands, but then, one day, they stopped waving and shaking and holding and started throwing. And, just like a stone, when you get hit by sin, it hurts. In God's eyes, all sins are the same whether they are thoughts, words, or actions. But for us, different sins may cause greater hurts. Some sins sting (like small stones), and other sins scar (like big, jagged stones). Can you think of a time when someone sinned against you?

Maybe it was your mom or your dad. They did something big like bailing on your family or abusing you or choosing a six-pack over you every night. Or maybe it was something small but endless like a controlling personality, constant criticism, or not teaching you what a healthy, affectionate, you-first relationship looks like. Or maybe it was someone at school. The kid who was willing to crush your spirit for the sake of a crude joke at your expense. The Snapchat story that embarrassed you so badly you wished you could move to a new school. Or maybe it was a relationship. The boy who only said sweet things because he wanted sex.

*When sin hits, it hurts.*

The girl so insecure that she would accuse and threaten and disrespect you. The husband who vowed before God that he would put you first no matter what . . . until his work got busy and the kids got crazy and real life got costly. The wife who assumed her marriage would be fine without truly prioritizing her husband.

Stones are thrown everywhere. A grouchy neighbor. A boss who plays favorites. A church that doesn't practice the love that it preaches. In-laws who forget their place in their children's decisions. From our perspective, sin can be big or small, one time or repetitive, a text or a tone, a word or an action, something you do or something you don't or something done to you. And when sin hits, it hurts. It wounds. It scars. That's why God hates it.

You probably are not shocked that God forgives us and wants us to forgive others. Jesus taught us to pray, "Our Father in heaven . . . forgive us our sins as we forgive those who sin against us." But what exactly does that mean? Should we just forgive and forget? What about consequences and boundaries? What if you cannot forgive yourself? What if you do not want to forgive them? How do you know that God truly forgives you? Those questions are what this book is all about.

—Mike Novotny

# you must choose to forgive every day

Let's start with the basics, with the four things you could do after sin hits you like a stone. There are four paths you could take, but there is only one that God wants you to take.

The first thing you could do after being sinned against is *forget*. That's what people say, right? "You need to forgive and . . . forget." Sounds like a nice Pinterest post, doesn't it? But is it biblical? We do know that when God forgives us, his forgiveness is so complete, thorough, and constant that it's *almost* like he forgot. God promised in Jeremiah 31:34, **"I will forgive their wickedness and remember their sins no more."** Wow. That is stunning and beautiful and life-giving, isn't it? So should you do the same? Don't remember it? Don't think about it? Just forgive and forget?

I searched the entire Bible looking for an answer to that question. I learned that the word *forget* is used 64 total times. Guess how many have to do with forgetting about someone else's sin? Zero. In fact, "forgive and forget" is a guilt-inducing, danger-producing way to live. To tell people they haven't truly forgiven until they've completely forgotten is a guarantee of guilt. Because how can you just forget? If that stone has left a scar, how can you not think about what happened? And sometimes you don't want to. In a later chapter, we're going to talk about consequences and boundaries, how a good memory can protect you and your church and your children from evil people who would love it if we all forgot about their behavior. You can forgive even if you don't forget.

Which brings us to the second thing you could do after being sinned against: *get back.* Payback. Vengeance. Settling the score. The thing about getting hit with a stone is that the stone drops at your feet, right there to grab and aim and fire back.

"You're going to raise your voice? I can too."

"You're going to call names? I can think of a few."

"You're going to criticize how I look, how I work, how I parent, how I serve you? Well, I have a list of things to say to you too."

Payback is part of the sinful human heart. No tutorials necessary. Since hurt people hurt people, stones rarely sit there for long.

But vengeance doesn't work. Just ask Samson and the Philistines. Do you know that Old Testament Bible history? Around 1100 B.C., an Israelite womanizer with supernatural strength named Samson got into a stone-throwing fest with the neighboring Philistines. First, the Philistines threatened to kill Samson's wife, so he killed 30 of their men. So they killed his wife and her dad. So he took the jagged jawbone of a donkey and covered the rocks with their blood. So they bribed his new lady friend, Delilah, into finding the secret of his strength and then gouged out Samson's eyes. So Samson tore down the temple where the Philistines gathered to mock him. They died. He died. The end. No matter how ugly or bloody it got, the score was never settled.

You won't settle the score either. If you make him/her/them hurt, it won't help. Hearts don't heal like that. An old Chinese proverb says, "The one who refuses to forgive should dig two graves." Or consider what Peter, Paul, and Jesus say: **"Do not repay evil with evil or insult with insult"** (1 Peter 3:9). **"Do not take revenge, my dear friends"** (Romans 12:19). **"You have heard that it was said, 'Love your neighbor and hate your enemy.' But I tell you, love your enemies"** (Matthew 5:43,44). Don't get them back. It won't work. It's not what God wants.

The third thing you could do after being sinned against is *get bitter.* Bitterness is when you pick up the stone and squeeze it, when you hold on to it so tightly that it starts to hold on to you. It's when you are so angry that you can't pray for that person, and you can't even imagine loving that person in any way. No, you're not going to throw a stone back at them, but you hope (secretly) that someone else does. You hope your ex gets dumped. You hope the trash-talker gets schooled. You hope they hurt just like they hurt you.

Twenty years ago, I did a lot of Weedwacking. My first job was doing lawn care at a condo complex/golf course, and every week there were hours and hours and hours of Weedwacking to be done. So I'd gas up the tank, grip the handle, and pull the trigger until the fuel ran out. But by the time it did, my hands could barely move. I had held on to the handle so tightly for so long that my fingers felt stuck in that position, and I had to pry them open.

Bitterness is like that. The longer you hold on to that stone, the harder it is to let it go, to fold your hands in prayer, and to open your hands in love. Getting bitter never makes it better. Hebrews 12:15 says, **"See to it that . . . no bitter root grows up to cause trouble and defile many."** Bitterness is a root that produces toxic fruit.

*God wants you and me to forgive.*

Which is why there is a fourth option, God's option, the thing that God wants you to do every time someone sins against you. Don't get back. Don't get bitter. Don't forget. No, God wants you and me *to forgive.*

Let's define that difficult word. *Forgiveness = the daily choice to let the stone alone.* Forgiveness is a choice. It's not something you feel but something you do. And you do it *daily.* You don't forgive once and move on. No, that stone is always there at your feet, which means every day, every moment, with every trigger, with every memory you have to make a choice. It isn't accurate to ask, "Have I forgiven him?" but rather, "Am I forgiving him? Right now, what am I doing? Am I trying to get him back? Am I consumed by bitterness? Or am I making the choice right now to let the stone alone? To leave the vengeance to the God who will come to judge the living and dead? To believe that God's got this too?"

Let's go back to Peter, Paul, and Jesus. **"Do not repay evil with evil or insult with insult. On the contrary, repay evil with blessing, because to this you were called so that you may inherit a blessing"** (1 Peter 3:9).

**"Bless those who persecute you; bless and do not curse"** (Romans 12:14). **"But I tell you, love your enemies and pray for those who persecute you"** (Matthew 5:44). This is forgiveness, the forgiveness that frees you from an endless life of insults, from a crazy cycle that will only make you sick, from bitterness that will swallow your heart whole. This is what you can do even if they are not sorry, even if it is not safe to see them, even if they have passed on.

Would you be willing to forgive? Not to act like nothing happened. Not to go back like things were before. But would you forgive today? Would you let that stone alone and have hands holy enough to pray, to bless, to love? At some point today, I'd like you to go outside and find a stone. I want you to take it inside and put it where you can see it. Use it to visualize what's happening in your heart. And then, with the help of a forgiving God, let it alone. Make the daily choice to let the stone alone, to forgive.

*Make the daily choice to let the stone alone.*

That's the beautiful thing that a man named Brandt did. In the fall of 2018, Botham Jean, a 26-year-old accountant, was sitting in his apartment watching football and eating ice cream when the unthinkable happened. Amber Guyger, a police officer, entered the apartment, believing it was her own in error and assuming Botham was a burglar. She shot and killed him. And threw a boulder at Botham's family. Thirteen months later, after Guyger was sentenced to ten years in prison, Botham's brother, Brandt, made a statement to his brother's murderer. "I hope you go to God with all the guilt," he told her. "I forgive you. I know if you go to God and ask him, he will forgive you. . . . I love you just like anyone else. . . . I personally want the best for you." And he encouraged her to find eternal life through Christ. But then Brandt did something supernatural. He asked the judge, "Can I give her a hug? Please. Please." And he did. For an entire minute, he hugged the woman who hurt his family so deeply. And if you watch the footage (search "Brandt Jean" on YouTube), you'll notice something about Brandt's hands as Amber collapsed into his arms. They were open. Because he let her stone alone.

You can too. But first you need to think of Jesus. The cross. The gospel. The God who let your stone alone. The God who was first in the forgiveness line. The God who, despite everything you've done, has no plans to pay you back. He forgives.

That's what Peter, Paul, and Jesus taught me. Peter wrote, **"When** [Jesus] **suffered, he made no threats. . . . He himself bore our sins in his body on the cross"** (1 Peter 2:23,24). Jesus was stronger than Samson, but he used his strength to save his enemies, not to slaughter them. He bore our sins on the cross. Paul agreed: **"Blessed are those whose transgressions are forgiven, whose sins are covered. Blessed is the one whose sin the Lord will never count against them"** (Romans 4:7,8). How blessed we are, how happy to know that it's all forgiven. Jesus' blood covers it all up. There is no sin that our Father picks up to punish us. Our Father's hands are open to bless us, to help us, to embrace us like that man in the courtroom. And the night before Jesus died, he took the cup and said, **"This is my blood of the covenant, which is poured out for many for the forgiveness of**

**sins"** (Matthew 26:28). His blood was poured out for us, the blood of the covenant, God's promise to forgive our wickedness and, somehow, remember our sins no more. I won't lie to you. Forgiveness is hard. But God is here to help. When you see that stone, remember our Father who forgives even our failure to forgive. Remember our Savior who turned the other cheek to shed his blood on the cross. Remember the Spirit who produces the fruit of kindness, gentleness, and love, even toward those who hurt us. And with divine help in your heart, choose to forgive, to let the stone alone.

# *for further study*

# YOU MUST CHOOSE TO FORGIVE *EVERY* DAY

*Pastor Ben Sadler*

According to Pastor Mike, forgiveness is one of the hardest things God calls us to do. We would like to move on, but deep wounds have a way of hanging around and disrupting our lives. In fact, Pastor Mike says our emotional and spiritual pain is like being hit with stones. Some sin may appear small and feel like little stones pelting us. But some sin may feel like getting hit by large, jagged rocks. And yet, even with such deep emotional pain, God calls us to forgive.

It's one thing to listen or read about forgiveness. It's another thing to choose to practice forgiveness. That's why in this study, we will take action as we learn to make the daily decision to forgive.

## Three dangerous things you can do with your "stone"

### 1. Forget

Instead of choosing to forgive, you might just *try to forget* about the sin committed against you. But is that possible? Are humans capable of forgetting what has happened to them? We do read in Jeremiah 31:34

that God says, **"For I will forgive their wickedness and will remember their sins no more."** But let me state the obvious, you are not God. Trying to forget the sins committed against you is like trying to keep a beach ball underwater. Those memories have a way of popping back up.

## Practice

Next time the hurt from sins committed against you pops up, don't try to force it back down and forget it. Let it come to the surface. Then breathe deeply as you pray to God to move you through this challenging moment. Use the space here to write your prayer down. (In addition, you might consider meditating on Psalm 23 or Exodus 14:14: **"The Lord will fight for you; you need only to be still."**)

_____

_____

_____

_____

_____

_____

_____

_____

_____

## Discuss or journal

Explain why this practice of prayer is more beneficial than trying to *forget* what happened to you.

_____

_____

_____

_____

_____

_____

_____

_____

_____

_____

_____

_____

_____

_____

## 2. Get back

Instead of choosing to forgive, you might try to *get back* at the person who wronged you. But revenge doesn't only hurt the person who hurt you. It's like throwing a stone that boomerangs back at you. Or as Nelson Mandela is said to have commented, "Resentment is like drinking poison and then hoping it will kill your enemies." That's why the apostle Paul commands us, **"Do not take revenge, my dear friends, but leave room for God's wrath"** (Romans 12:19). Let God handle justice according to his will.

## Practice

Identify and write down the times you tried to get revenge.

_____

_____

_____

_____

_____

_____

_____

_____

## Discuss or journal

Explain what happened as a result of getting revenge. Did your situation get better or worse?

_____

_____

_____

_____

_____

_____

_____

_____

_____

_____

_____

_____

_____

_____

## 3. Get bitter

Instead of choosing to forgive, you might try *getting bitter*. Pastor Mike explains that getting back and getting bitter are very similar. But here is the difference. Getting back means you throw the stone. Getting bitter means you hold on to it. Just think about what it would be like to carry around a heavy, jagged stone everywhere you went. That's what you are doing when you hold on to bitterness. That's why the Bible says, **"[Let] no bitter root grow up to cause trouble and defile many"** (Hebrews 12:15).

### Practice

Identify where in your body you can "feel" bitterness. Is it a tightness in the stomach? Is it in your head as you ruminate on your pain?

## Discuss or journal

What are some signs that you still have bitterness in your heart? In what ways is bitterness unhelpful for your heart and soul?

# Learning to make the daily decision to forgive

Pastor Mike defined *forgiveness* as "the daily choice to let the stone alone." This doesn't mean we are forced to forget it. It just means we are not going to pick up the stone of sin and either throw it back or carry it around.

But then maybe we wonder: "If I don't do something about the sin I suffered, who will?"

God will. God promises to be the final judge.

## Practice

Read and meditate on Romans 12:17-19: **"Do not repay anyone evil for evil. Be careful to do what is right in the eyes of everyone. If it is possible, as far as it depends on you, live at peace with everyone. Do not take revenge, my dear friends, but leave room for God's wrath, for it is written: 'It is mine to avenge; I will repay,' says the Lord."** Journal your thoughts here:

_____

_____

_____

_____

_____

_____

## Discuss or journal

Paul says that God will be the judge. Therefore, we are free to let the stone alone, bless, and even love our enemy. What would it look like for you to follow what Paul teaches about love and forgiveness?

Pastor Mike emphasizes that forgiveness is not a feeling we wait for but a choice we need to make every day. That might sound like an exhausting and even overwhelming daily habit. But that's why we need to be filled up with God's love and forgiveness through the Holy Spirit.

## Practice

Read, meditate, and jot down your thoughts on the following passages.

> ***Bear with each other and forgive one another
> if any of you has a grievance against someone.
> Forgive as the Lord forgave you.***
>
> Colossians 3:13

### *We love because he first loved us.*

1 John 4:19

**Therefore, I tell you, her many sins have been forgiven—as her great love has shown. But whoever has been forgiven little loves little.**

Luke 7:47

**I am the vine; you are the branches. If you remain in me and I in you, you will bear much fruit; apart from me you can do nothing.**

John 15:5

## Discuss or journal

List how you can be filled up with God's love and forgiveness through the Holy Spirit so that you can forgive
your enemy.

_____

_____

_____

_____

_____

_____

_____

_____

_____

_____

_____

_____

_____

Finally, Pastor Mike encourages us to watch the video of Brandt Jean forgiving Amanda Guyger. Guyger murdered Jean's brother, Botham, after she mistakenly entered the wrong apartment and thought an intruder was in her living room. At her trial, Brandt Jean not only forgave her for her sin in Jesus' name but embraced her with a minute-long hug. You can find the video on YouTube (search "Brandt Jean").

### Discuss or journal

Why do you find this video so moving? What do Brandt's actions teach you about Jesus and forgiveness?

# when forgiving feels impossible

You and I probably agree that forgiveness is a good thing. When someone sins against us, when they throw a stone that hurts us, we know we shouldn't repress it and forget it. Or pick up the stone for vengeance. Or hold on to that stone in bitterness. No, it's best to forgive, to make the daily choice to let the stone alone. That's good for God, for us, and for them.

But when forgiveness is a choice you have to make when you're hurting, that's insanely hard. I have yet to be deeply wounded in life, but I can remember throwing stones with a fellow Christian a few years ago. She wasn't being loving toward me, and I wasn't very loving in return. So eventually we met face-to-face to figure it out. What I remember most about that conversation is when we talked about what God would want—humility and love—she closed her eyes and gave a slow nod, "I know. I know." I knew exactly how she felt. Love people, even your enemies—I know that. Bless those who curse you—I know that. Forgive—I know that too. But to do that when emotions are high and when you still hurt is so hard.

Do you feel that too? Maybe you've been through way worse than I have from your parents or your kids or your classmates or your church or your spouse or the system or your ex or whomever. Did you find it hard to actually forgive them? to make that daily choice?

If so, I am really glad you're reading this, because out of the 128 Bible passages that mention this idea, many of them tell us God's key to forgiveness. In this chapter I want to focus on two of those passages from the lips of Jesus himself, one in a prayer that he taught and another in a story that he told.

Let's start with the prayer. You might have heard it before—the Lord's Prayer. Not only does the prayer say, "Father . . . your will be done" (such as forgiving people) and "lead us not into temptation" (such as not into bitterness) and "deliver us from evil" (such as the evil of vengeance), but right in the middle of the prayer we find words specifically about forgiveness. Jesus taught us to pray, **"We also forgive everyone who sins against us"** (Luke 11:4). Boom. There it is. We forgive. Everyone. When someone hurts you, when they owe you, when they sin against you, don't take vengeance or give into bitterness. No, Jesus taught you and me to talk to God about forgiving everyone.

But do you know what Jesus said first? Let me show you the whole verse: **"Forgive us *our sins*, for we also forgive everyone who sins against us."** "First, Father, forgive my sins. God, please forgive my sins. Lord, don't pick up my stones. Don't pay me back for what I've done wrong." Jesus implied that the offensive but beautiful choice of forgiveness starts not with you and them but with you and God.

That's what changed Jean Valjean. If you ever want to see me get choked up (and possibly ugly cry), buy me a ticket to see the Broadway musical *Les Misérables*. Ever heard of it? It's about this petty thief named Jean Valjean who refuses to forgive the system that hurt him and lives with a bitter root squeezing the goodness out of his heart. Homeless and with nowhere to go, a local priest opens the church for him to stay, but Valjean, in his dark spiral, decides to steal some silver candlesticks and run away into the night. The police catch him, ready to bring the hammer of justice down on his head, but the priest defends him, claiming the candlesticks were a gift. Stunned, Valjean stands there, unsure what to say, until the priest draws close to his ear and says in a low voice, "Jean Valjean, my brother, you no longer belong to evil but to good. . . . I withdraw [your soul] from black thoughts and . . . give it to God." And that moment, that forgiveness, frees Valjean. It changes him.

*Jesus leans in close.*

It changes us too. Like that priest, Jesus has shown us grace. When justice would have locked us up in hell, far from God, Jesus leans in close and whispers, "I forgive you. I have redeemed you. I bled to buy you back and give you to God." So when Jesus taught us to pray something seemingly impossible—"We forgive everyone"—he knew where to start . . . with the forgiveness that found us first.

Ah, but here's a big, big question—When you look at his cross, how much forgiveness do you see? How many of your stones sit beneath his feet? Your honest answer matters. **"Whoever has been forgiven little loves little"** (Luke 7:47). That's what Jesus said. But the one who has been forgiven much . . . they know how to forgive.

That's why Jesus didn't just teach us a prayer; he also told us a story. In Matthew chapter 18, Jesus laid out the steps for dealing with sin in the church, which made Peter, one of Jesus' friends, ask a question: "Um, Jesus, how many times do I have to forgive?"

Here's the story that Jesus *almost* told—Once upon a time there was a man who owed the king one hundred silver coins. But he didn't have the money, so he begged the king for mercy. The king paused, smiled, and said, "I forgive you. I forgive your debt, all one hundred coins. Go. We're good." So the forgiven man left, ecstatic over the king's forgiveness. Until he ran into a neighbor, the guy who also owed him one hundred coins. He grabbed the neighbor and demanded payment, and the man begged for mercy. Unlike the king, however, there was no smile, no go in peace, no forgiveness. He threw the man in prison until the entire debt was paid. And when the king heard what the man had done, the man who had just been forgiven that very amount, he was royally ticked.

That was the story Jesus *almost* told. Except for one little detail—do you know the story well enough to know what it was? In Jesus' story, the first man didn't owe the king one hundred silver coins. No, here's what Jesus actually said: **"The kingdom of heaven is like a king who wanted to settle accounts with his servants. As he began the settlement, a man who owed him *ten thousand bags of gold* was brought to him"** (Matthew 18:23,24). The debt was not silver but gold. Not coins but bags. Not one hundred but ten thousand. It's hard to perfectly crunch the numbers, but scholars suggest the man owed the king seven billion dollars and the man was owed twelve thousand dollars. Seven billion to twelve thousand. If my math is right, that's not 10% of his debt or 1% of his debt or .1% or .01% or .001% but .00017% of what the king forgave. His debt was one million times worse than the debt owed to him.

What was Jesus trying to say in his story? He was saying, "You know that person who hurt you? You know that stone that's so hard to let alone? What do you think? Are you as

43

bad as them?" Jesus says, "You're a million times worse. A million." When you say to someone, "How could you? I would never do something like that!" Well, you did. A lot. When you say, "Why would you make our lives so messy? Why would you do this to our family?" You should know exactly why because it's what you've done a million times to God. Jesus knows we get so infatuated with the stones thrown at us that we forget something. We focus so much on every edge, every detail of what someone did to us that we lose sight of how often we have done the exact same thing to God. How many of your stones sit beneath Jesus' feet? It's like buckets and buckets and buckets of stones.

*How many of your stones sit at Jesus' feet?*

You and I can't forget that. If you turn your back on every sin you've committed and only think about what your ex did, what your dad did, what your boyfriend did, what your boss did, it is the craziest hypocrisy in the world. And the craziest part is that every sin you have ever committed is against God. He's holy and good, and he's been so kind to you every day of your life and yet, every time you worry, every time you lash out, every time you want to get your way, every time you forget his rules, you throw a stone at God. If you excuse your past and your sin, that person who sinned against you will be the villain. You will feel so superior and spend your days judging them and wanting consequences and pointing your finger at them because of the consequences. But you don't want God to do that to you, do you?

I know this might seem absurd to you, someone who's been sinned against, who's hurting, whose life may have been T-boned by someone else's evil, but Jesus knows that until you and I do the math and honestly believe we are the worst sinners in the room, we'll be stuck, unable to let the stone alone.

Once that sinks in, there is something else I want you to see in Jesus' story. **"The servant's master took pity on him, canceled the debt and let him go"** (Matthew 18:27). The king let him go. He cancelled the debt. Not one hundred silver coins but ten thousand bags of gold. That's like seven billion dollars gone. Which is Jesus' way of saying, "God forgives a lot." When we pray, "Our Father . . . forgive us our sins," he does. A lot. He's not the God of second chances but the God who forgives billions. Billions!

I did the math. Seven billion divided by the average life span is 88,607,594 sins/year. Or 242,760 sins/day. Or 10,115 sins/hour. Or 168 sins/minute. Or 3 sins/second. Every second for your entire life! That is what the King of love is willing to forgive and remember no more. *God let your (seven billion) stones alone!*

This is what Jesus did for you and me. God piled every one of your sins at the cross and then nailed down the hands of his Son so not a single stone would be thrown, so the King would let every stone alone, and so his hands would be open to pray, "Father, forgive them!" Despite the consequences, there would be no condemnation. Not for you or me. Not for anyone who trusts in Jesus.

Did you know the words of "Amazing Grace" were inspired by a famously sinful pastor? In the late 1700s, John Newton was the captain of a slave ship. When God opened his eyes to the wretchedness of his sin, he was amazed that grace would even forgive a wretch like him (that's why he wrote "Amazing Grace"). But he also wrote this—"Are you not amazed that you should have so much as a hope, that, poor and needy as you are, the Lord thinks of you? But let not [your sin] discourage you; for . . . if [God] casts none out who come to him, why should you fear? Our sins are great— but his righteousness is greater" (https://www.gracegems. org/Newton/001.htm).

So as you make the daily choice to let that stone alone, I pray you remember not just how much you've sinned but how much you've been forgiven.

*for further study*

# WHEN FORGIVING FEELS IMPOSSIBLE

*Pastor Ben Sadler*

Jesus taught his followers to pray the Lord's Prayer. It is a beautiful prayer that calls upon God our Father to rule over us and let his will be done among us. Also, we ask for daily bread and daily deliverance. But right in the middle of the prayer is a request for forgiveness. Jesus taught us to pray:

**Forgive us our sins, for we also forgive everyone who sins against us.**

Luke 11:4

Those words are not only challenging, but they are also downright offensive. I think we would have preferred if Jesus said, "Forgive us our sins and help us to forgive others." But that's not what he said. He taught us to pray, "Lord, treat me as I treat others. Lord, be as gracious and forgiving to me as I am to others."

Why would Jesus teach us to pray this way? Well, Pastor Mike says that Jesus wants us to remember how much we have been forgiven first before we attempt to forgive others. God wants us to consider the mountain of sins that we have committed against God and his abundant forgiveness before we look at the stones that have been thrown at us.

But how do we do that? Jesus taught a story to help us visualize God's grace to us so we might learn how we can be gracious and forgiving to others. Let's take a deeper dive into that story as we apply the lessons from Pastor Mike to our lives.

### First, consider our debt to God

In Matthew 18:23-35, Jesus told a story about a servant who owed his master ten thousand bags of gold. Pastor Mike said that some scholars believe this was the equivalent of seven billion dollars. Jesus wanted us to see ourselves in a similar situation before God. Our daily impure thoughts, words, and actions are accruing an unpayable debt before God.

### Discuss or journal

Pastor Mike talks about our sins being like a pile of stones at Jesus' feet. What would it be like if we could see every one of our sins as stones laid in front of us? How big would our mountain of stones be? What would it feel like to see a visual of our sins?

_____

_____

_____

_____

In Jesus' story, the servant begged to have his debt forgiven, and surprisingly the master granted his request. He forgave all his debt, just like that. The Bible says that is exactly what God has done for us. He has forgiven our mountain of sins because Jesus paid for all of them on the cross.

### Discuss or journal

If you were to put yourself in Jesus' story and were the one who had received forgiveness for a seven-billion-dollar debt, how would you feel? In a way, that's exactly what happened. God has forgiven you of your billions of sins. Describe how you feel when such a reality sinks into your heart?

## Second, extend forgiveness to others

In Jesus' story there was a surprise ending. After the servant left his master's presence, he found one of his fellow servants who owed him something like a few thousand dollars. It was a substantial debt but nothing close to his debt to his master. Instead of forgiving his fellow servant's debt, he threw him into prison until he paid back every last penny. Through this story, Jesus was showing us how forgetful we can all be. We forget how gracious God has been to us, so we don't extend that kind of grace to others.

## Discuss or journal

In what ways has this kind of forgetfulness shown up in your life? Describe a time when you withheld forgiveness from someone. Explain why it is so easy for us to forget how God has been so gracious and forgiving to us.

At the end of the story, the master threw the unmerciful servant into prison because he had not shown his fellow servant the same kind of forgiveness that he had experienced. Then Jesus closed his story with these words: **"This is how my heavenly Father will treat each of you unless you forgive your brother and sister from your heart"** (Matthew 18:35). Jesus was teaching us that if we don't extend forgiveness to others, it shows that we don't know and believe the forgiveness that God has extended to us. But when we show forgiveness to others, it is a reminder to our hearts of God's grace to us.

## Practice

Consider making the Lord's Prayer a daily practice. Not only will this prayer teach you to pray for God's will and deliverance from your enemies, but you will be reminded to forgive others daily as you have been forgiven.

*Our Father in heaven,*
*hallowed be your name,*
*your kingdom come,*
*your will be done*
*on earth as in heaven.*
*Give us today our daily bread.*
*Forgive us our sins,*
*as we forgive those*
*who sin against us.*
*Lead us not into temptation,*
*but deliver us from evil.*
*For the kingdom, the power,*
*and the glory are yours*
*now and forever. Amen.*

# I forgave. Now how do I heal?

Forgiveness. It's what God wants you to do when someone sins against you. When someone throws a stone and it hits and hurts, God doesn't want you to just forget about it or throw it back in vengeance or hold on to it in bitterness. No, he wants you to make the daily choice to let the stone alone, to forgive. Why? How? Because God started it! Because of Jesus, God doesn't get back or get bitter at believers; he just forgives all your sins, even if you're the sinner who's thrown seven billion stones. That's why Jesus taught us to pray, "Father, forgive us our sins as we forgive those who sin against us."

But there's still a big question we haven't covered yet—What then? So you make the choice to forgive, but what then? Do you just sit and wait for time to heal your wounds? Do you go back to the way things were before that person threw the stone? What does God want you to do while you forgive?

I bet you've felt this. You had that close friend whom you confided in. But then she didn't honor your trust. She shared your story, threw a stone. When it hit, it hurt. You're trying to forgive, but you want some space. You don't text her much anymore or want to grab coffee and talk. Are you holding on to bitterness? Or just healing?

Or you're dating a guy who has anger issues. He snaps when things don't go his way, but he's always sorry after. You don't want to be bitter, but you're not sure if you should stay with him. If you insist on counseling, are you making your love conditional? If you end the relationship, are you treating him in a way you don't want God to treat you?

Or what if someone you love drinks too much? They missed work (again) or can't pay the rent (again) and need a hand (again). Do you forgive? If not, are you holding on to the past? Don't you want God to be endlessly generous with you?

Or you're texting your ex about the kids' schedules and your ex is being . . . your ex. And you're not exactly inspired to say, "You first!" Are you being bitter? Or is that behavior just what happens after everything that's happened? Or so much more.

After her infidelity is exposed, after you find porn on his phone, after you end up in court, after your kid lies to you or a coworker steals from you, after whatever sin, things feel different. Things aren't the same. It's harder to love like before. So you ask, "Am I being bitter? Am I really forgiving?"

The apostle Paul, a Christian who wrote some of the Bible's best stuff on forgiveness, gives us a brilliant answer. Check out his words in Romans chapter 12:

**Bless those who persecute you; bless and do not curse. Rejoice with those who rejoice; mourn with those who mourn. Live in harmony with one another. Do not be proud, but be willing to associate with people of low position. Do not be conceited.**

**Do not repay anyone evil for evil. Be careful to do what is right in the eyes of everyone. If it is possible, as far as it depends on you, live at peace with everyone. Do not take revenge, my dear friends, but leave room for God's wrath, for it is written: "It is mine to avenge; I will repay," says the Lord. On the contrary:**

**"If your enemy is hungry, feed him; if he is thirsty, give him something to drink. In doing this, you will heap burning coals on his head."**

**Do not be overcome by evil, but overcome evil with good.** (verses 14-21)

Paul knows what happens—People sin. They do evil. They hurt you and me. But in the midst of that, here's God's goal—*Live at peace with everyone.* Paul takes us a step beyond forgiveness. God's goal is for you to live at peace *with everyone.*

How do you do that? Paul points to a few vital truths. First, he says, don't be proud. When someone's sin hits you or me, pride can pop up like a purple bruise. It's the pride that forgets about all our own stones, maybe even the stones we threw at them. About 1% of the time, like in cases of abuse, sin is one-sided. But the other 99% of the time, two sinners are involved in the situation:

- He got angry, but I was being pretty critical.

- My son is rebellious, but I have been working more than giving him my time and attention.

- She threw this massive stone in our marriage, but I threw a thousand small ones first.

Living at peace starts with humility, with owning our part. It's so hard to be humble when we're hurt. But Paul knows that humility is the path to healing.

Second, Paul urges—do good. Paul doesn't say, "Just let the stone alone and wait for healing." No, he repeatedly commands, "Bless those who persecute you. Rejoice when your sinner celebrates. Mourn when they suffer. Feed your stone thrower when she's hungry. Give that rock chucker something to drink when he's thirsty. Overcome the evil they did to you by doing good to them." Use your stone-free hands to love them.

*Humility is the path to healing.*

Unless you're in a really dangerous situation like going back to a person who abused you and put you in danger, what Paul wants you to do with a person who really annoys you and hurts you and bothers you is to serve them. Because here's what God knows. God knows that when a stone hits you and you're trying to leave it alone, if you don't occupy your hands with good, it will be almost impossible not to hold on to the past. And Paul says as soon as that stone hits, as fast as you can, you need to use those hands to bless people and to pray for people and to serve people who hurt you. Healing rarely happens just with waiting it out. The holy and hard way that God heals your hurts is by having you serve your enemies.

God knows that you and I don't do well with empty hands. In my experience, this is where people get stuck and stay hurt for way too long. Sin has separated them and smashed their intimacy and affection, so they wait until they feel better. But God calls us to serve the very ones who sinned against us. Healing happens faster when we're praying for God to make *them* better. This isn't easy (understatement of the decade)!

It's like physical therapy after surgery. No one wants to do it, but it's vital. So when sin happens, as soon as possible, start to pray for the person who wronged you. Ask God to bless them. What hurts the most, what feels the hardest, is the holy thing God uses to heal.

I got an email the other day from a guy at church who did this. He gave me permission to share his words: "Last week I started to pray that God would reach [my ex] and bring all the good to her that can only come from bringing the light to the darkness. . . . Since I have done that, my attitude toward her has changed. To the point where I am no longer holding that stone ready to throw it at her if needed. I have put the stone down. . . . Here's to stones down, heads up, and moving forward in freedom." I love that. Freedom. That's what forgiveness does. It frees us from bitterness. It helps us live at peace.

So what could you do to love them? What would be pure grace if you did it? What would offend the angry folks in "your corner," make God smile, and confuse your enemy to no end? What would love look like this week?

Aren't stories like that a glimpse of what happened with us and God? God didn't just let our stones alone, didn't forgive us and get on with his life. No, he loved us when we were his enemies. He restored the relationship, extended his hand, invited us to the table. Paul wrote, **"[God] has reconciled you by Christ's physical body through death to present you holy in his sight, without blemish and free from accusation"** (Colossians 1:22). The death of Jesus reconciles us to God, drawing us into his presence, where he smiles and blesses and loves. Even sinners like us can say, "GOD is here." Because he doesn't just forgive. He loves us.

This is what Paul urges us to imitate. Live at peace with everyone. Forgive and bless and serve and be living, breathing examples that sin doesn't have to separate us forever. Just like it didn't with Jesus.

But . . . Paul isn't ignorant. He knows that sometimes living at peace is not that simple. In fact, sometimes it's not even possible. Look at Romans 12:18 again: **"If it is possible, as far as it depends on you, live at peace with everyone."** *Hmm.* Paul knows you can't always live at peace with everyone. He lists two reasons why.

First, Paul says, **"As far as it depends on you."** Sometimes reconciliation isn't possible because it doesn't just depend on you. Restoring a relationship depends on . . . y'all—you and the person who threw the stone. How do they feel about what happened? What's their attitude toward their actions, toward God, toward you? Are they sorry? What kind of sorry are they? Watch out, wisdom says. Be shrewd, Jesus warned. Don't become a Christian doormat with no brains or boundaries. Forgiveness is a you thing. But living at peace is a y'all thing. Sometimes you should keep your distance from dangerous people. Sometimes you should end a friendship because he's a fool who doesn't want to learn from his mistakes. Sometimes you need to find a new church because they don't see the problem with their pride. Sometimes not-so-sorry sinners snap, "I'm sorry, okay," but they don't want to change or work on it or prove how sorry they are. So if you don't stick around and live at peace, that's not bitterness. Some things just don't depend on you.

Second, Paul admits, **"If it is possible."** Sometimes the consequences of sin are so bad, the trauma from the stone so severe, that it's not possible to go back. If you were a runner who got hit by a truck, you might not be able to run again, not like before, even after all the rehab and therapy. The same is true relationally. Some sins are so "big" that they change things between people.

Jesus knew that. In Matthew 5:24, Jesus taught on reconciliation. He said that if things are tense between you and another person, you should go fix it and try to live at peace with that person. But just eight verses later, Jesus admitted that it's not always possible. He was teaching about divorce and mentioned the stone of infidelity and how much it can hurt. Some couples can and do get through that. But others can't. Even if the one cheated on forgives and continues to serve and love and do good. Sometimes sin just changes things like trust. It's not always possible to go back like before.

That's true in other situations too. Like trusting a friend. Trust is like a tree; it takes a long time to grow.

Gossip or lies or betrayal can cut down the trees of trust in a day. And you can forgive, but you can't just regrow those trees. You might still love that person. You still forgive them. You're praying for God to bless them. But the nature of that sin might make things different than they were before. Sometimes it's just not possible.

But that doesn't have to leave you bitter. I learned that a few years ago at a wedding I did. The photographer was snapping pictures of the groom and the bride, laughing as they posed. "How do you know the couple?" I asked.

"Oh, she's one of my best friends, and he is . . . my ex-husband."

What?!? She must have read the expression on my face because she explained what happened, why they divorced, and how they chose forgiveness over bitterness. And it was beautiful!

So, let's summarize Paul's teaching:

### Step 1
They sin. They hit you and hurt you.

### Step 2
You look to God. You remember how he
let your seven billion stones alone.

### Step 3
You forgive. You make the daily choice
to let the stone alone.

### Step 4
You love. You pray and bless and feed and
serve the sinner, doing everything you can.

## Step 5

Y'all reconcile, if possible. If it's not possible
or if they aren't willing to change, you pray.
From a distance, you pray for God to change
their heart and bless them.

Now before I wrap up this chapter, doesn't this whole topic make you thankful for Jesus? Sometimes that relationship can't be saved, but this relationship always is. Our sin can mess up life with them, but it cannot separate us from him, not when we come to God through Jesus. Yes, we might mourn what sin has taken away, but nothing can separate us from the love of God that is in Christ Jesus. Because with God, all things are possible.

That is God's way to let go of the bitter and to make things better.

# *for further study*

# I FORGAVE.
# NOW HOW DO I HEAL?

*Pastor Ben Sadler*

So far we have seen that forgiveness is not a feeling; it is a daily choice to let "the stone" alone. We also have learned that we will be empowered to forgive when we recognize God's great forgiveness for us. But now what? After we have forgiven someone, how do we move on and heal? How do we live in the present and not ruminate on the past? How do we look to our future with hope and optimism?

The answers to these questions are challenging and nuanced. Pastor Mike says there are times when a person can only heal if they stay away from the person who hurt them. Maybe the person is abusive and continues to manipulate and control. Maybe the person is hardened in their sin and reconciling with them would enable more bad behavior. Yet sometimes healing comes when a person blesses and serves those who have wronged them. Doing good to the person who wronged them helps them to "let the stone alone" and move on.

So how does a person heal after they have forgiven the person who wronged them? Let's reread what Paul said about forgiveness and healing when he wrote to the Romans:

**Bless those who persecute you; bless and do not curse. Rejoice with those who rejoice; mourn with those who mourn. Live in harmony with one another. Do not be proud, but be willing to associate with people of low position. Do not be conceited.**

**Do not repay anyone evil for evil. Be careful to do what is right in the eyes of everyone. If it is possible, as far as it depends on you, live at peace with everyone. Do not take revenge, my dear friends, but leave room for God's wrath, for it is written: "It is mine to avenge; I will repay," says the Lord. On the contrary:**

**"If your enemy is hungry, feed him; if he is thirsty, give him something to drink. In doing this, you will heap burning coals on his head."**

**Do not be overcome by evil, but overcome evil with good.** (12:14-21)

### In some cases, we are called to bless

Paul knew what it felt like to be wronged. He had experienced being hurt and harmed by his fellow people. And yet he responded with love, and he called us to follow his example. Paul taught us to bless, feed, care, and love those who have hurt us.

Why? Because loving our enemies will allow us to heal. Pastor Mike says it this way: "God knows that when this stone hits you and you're trying to leave it alone, if you don't occupy your hands with good, it will be almost impossible not to hold on to the past. . . . The holy and hard way that God heals your hurts is by having you serve your enemies."

## Discuss or journal

Do you agree with Pastor Mike? Do you believe that if you don't love and serve your enemy that you will struggle to heal? Why or why not?

_____

_____

_____

_____

_____

_____

_____

_____

_____

_____

# Practice

Pray and bless one of your enemies today. Consider doing something good for them. Send a note. Write a post on social media. Help them in some way. Put some ideas down here.

## In some cases, we are called to stay away

Paul said, "*IF* it is possible, as far as it depends on you, live at peace with everyone." Paul knew that it was not always a possibility to live at peace with everyone. Reconciliation only happens when both sides are following what God says. You might forgive someone, but if that person is a manipulator, dangerous, or is showing no signs of repentance, the wise decision is to stay away.

Jesus once described some people as wolves. Then he said, **"Therefore be as shrewd as snakes and as innocent as doves"** (Matthew 10:16). In other words, you will not heal if you continue to put yourself back into danger.

## Discuss or journal

List the circumstances when it would not be wise to return to someone who has wronged you.

## Practice

Identify the people whom you believe you should stay away from.

## In some cases, it's not up to you

Pastor Mike mentions that there are some cases where the situation is irreversible. As far as it depended on you, you tried to change, forgive, and reconcile, but it just wasn't possible. Even in those cases, Pastor Mike says you don't need to be bitter. You can keep your focus on Jesus as you wait for his return, when he will reconcile all things in heaven and on earth under his kingdom.

## Discuss or journal

How can a person live in peace even when they face an irreversible situation?

_____

_____

_____

_____

_____

_____

_____

_____

_____

_____

## Practice

Consider where you still hold on to bitterness. Give it up to God and let him be the final judge. Write a prayer asking him to help you let go of bitterness.

_____

_____

_____

_____

_____

_____

_____

_____

_____

_____

_____

_____

_____

## As far as it depends on Jesus, nothing can separate you from his love

Relationships can be beautiful and life giving, but they can also be challenging, messy, and even destructive. But Pastor Mike points us back to the only relationship that will be completely stable. We have a promise from God that nothing can separate us from his love (Romans 8:39).

## Discuss or journal

List the ways your relationship with God is different from all other relationships that you experience.

_____

_____

_____

_____

_____

_____

_____

_____

_____

_____

## Practice

Read, meditate, and jot down your thoughts on Romans 8:37-39:

**No, in all these things we are more than conquerors through him who loved us. For I am convinced that neither death nor life, neither angels nor demons, neither the present nor the future, nor any powers, neither height nor depth, nor anything else in all creation, will be able to separate us from the love of God that is in Christ Jesus our Lord.**

# *I can't forgive myself*

If it offends you, then you get it. That's how I would summarize what God says about forgiveness. Nothing about it feels "right." When someone sins against you, when they don't love you, when they throw a stone and hurt you, forgiveness insists on leaving the stone alone, which offends our sense of justice. And forgiveness looks up to God and admits that we've thrown even more stones, which offends our sense of goodness. And forgiveness says that we are forgiven for all of it, every single stone, which offends our sense of worthiness. And forgiveness says, "Now go bless them, pray for them, serve them, love them—yes, them!" which offends our sense of fairness. None of it's natural, but it is beautiful and powerful. As we wrap up this book on forgiveness, I want to talk about a feeling and a phrase that comes up all the time in our lives—*forgive yourself*.

Did you know that at my church, lots of people argue with the pastors? Here's what happens:

An email shows up. "Pastor, can we talk? Soon?"

A person shows up at the office door, too embarrassed to make eye contact. We sit down and I say, "What's going on?"

Then the person says, "I messed up. I lied. I hid. I clicked. I strayed. I yelled. I relapsed. I'm such an idiot."

"Okay," I respond, "thank you for telling me. I know that stuff is hard to say out loud. Let's talk about what to do next, but first there's something really important I need to tell you. In fact, if there's only one thing you remember about this conversation, I want it to be this. You ready?" And the person nods. So I open to a passage, one that seems best for the specific sin, and I read, "If we confess our sins, God is faithful . . . and he will purify us from all unrighteousness." And I smile, "Isn't that word amazing? All unrighteousness. All the stuff that's not right. The thing you just said that was not right. God forgives that. Jesus died to purify you from that." And I smile even bigger and wait for a reaction.

And that's when some people argue with the pastor: "But I messed up. But I can't believe I . . . But I just can't forgive myself."

*I can't forgive myself.* That feeling is all too frequent in life. Sometimes you sin, you throw a stone, and it hits someone and hurts them badly. But then you can't let the stone alone. You pick it up and hold on to the past with bitter regret. You grip it tightly and hit yourself with self-loathing vengeance. You stay up at night trying to make sense of it—"What was I thinking? Why didn't I see that? Why did I do that?"

That lack of forgiveness can happen to any of us over anything, but it most often happens due to three factors.

First, when you're close. When you sin against

someone close (your kid, your girlfriend, your husband, your roommate), you see how bad sin is. You can type something nasty in the comment section, but you can't see the damage. But you can when you're close. You realize that words can really hurt people; they can ring in their ears for years. So when you told your mom you hated her, called him that name just to make him hurt, threw the past back in her face just to win the argument, you see how ugly sin is. It's hard to forgive yourself.

Second, when you are compassionate. The dark part of having a big heart is that you'll break when they're broken. You care about people so much that you hate yourself so much for hurting them. Your addiction cost them so much time, so much worry, so many sleepless nights. It's hard to forgive yourself.

Finally, when there are consequences. When your drive at work left your kid closer to the day care provider than you, when your son grew up hearing more of Siri's voice than yours, when your attitude made the situation so tense, it's hard to forgive yourself. Combine two or all three of those, and you have a recipe for holding on to your own stone.

So what do you do when you're holding on to the past, when you can't forgive yourself? God's answer is amazing . . . and amazingly offensive. You want to hear it? Okay, I warned you.

*A lack of self-forgiveness is pure arrogance.* You might feel humble when you hold on to that stone, but you aren't. In fact, when you won't forgive yourself, you are acting more arrogant than ever before.

First, because you think way too much about yourself. Let me explain. If you want to feel unworthy of God's acceptance, too messed up for him to love, too far gone to be forgiven, why didn't you start sooner? Why was it that sin seven months ago or that stone you threw three years ago? Why didn't you go back before that? Some of you grew up in churches where you confessed every week, "I am altogether sinful from birth," so why not start back then?

Here's the answer—because you didn't think you were that bad. Maybe you didn't believe that how you behaved B.S. (Before that Stone) was all that bad. You said you were a sinner. You confessed that you needed the cross. But maybe, deep down, you thought you deserved God.

Here's what I'd say—If you think that sin can separate you from God, then don't stop there. Don't limit it to adultery or addiction or some idiotic decision. Be honest about it. Then don't forgive yourself for speeding on the interstate. Or worrying about Grandma's cancer. Or finding your self-worth in your weight. Or "just looking" twice at her in the mirrors at the gym. Or venting about your coworkers after work. If you want to take sin that seriously, fine. But then do it right. Refuse to forgive yourself for all of it. Don't be arrogant enough to think you were good with God before that happened.

This is what shocks me about King David. Years ago when I was in Israel, I took a picture from about the place where David, an ancient king, looked down from his palace and locked his eyes on a bathing woman and lusted after her. The story is bad—he wanted her and, as the king, he got what he wanted. She ended up pregnant with the king's baby, a B.C. story for TMZ, but David managed to kill her husband and cover it all up. Eventually, the truth came out—all the stones that this "good king" threw—and David wrote a song to express how sorry he was. But listen to what he said, **"Have mercy on me, O God, according to your unfailing love. . . . Surely I was sinful at birth, sinful from the time my mother conceived me"** (Psalm 51:1,5). Did you catch that? David said, "God, I need your mercy. I need your unfailing love. Because I was sinful. Not from the first thought of sex but from the moment my mother conceived me." David didn't think his sin started with that famous stone. We shouldn't either.

Second (sorry, the offensive part isn't over yet), refusing to forgive yourself is pure arrogance because you think way too little about God. Imagine if you weren't sitting down with the pastor but with our Father and his Son, your Savior.

"I'm so sorry, God," you confess.

"I know. But I forgive you."

"Well, thanks, God, but I just can't forgive myself."

"Okay, but I'm God . . . the King, the Lord, the One who gets the last word, and I forgive you."

"Sure, but I really feel . . ."

So, Jesus jumps in. "Look at these scars. Here is the proof. I died for you. For that. It is finished. All of it is finished. That stone is finished."

"Gee, Jesus, that's nice of you, but I just don't know if it's really finished. It wouldn't be right just to move on, you know?"

> *Refusing to forgive yourself is pure arrogance.*

Do you see? If God says you are forgiven, then not forgiving yourself is telling the Righteous One he's wrong! He's the one true God! You are one of 7.8 billion people who probably can't remember your brother's phone number from memory. He's God! He knows what he's doing, what he's saying, and exactly what he's forgiving.

So that's the problem. A lack of forgiveness is pure arrogance. But I've saved the most offensive part for last. You ready for it? I hope so, because it's offensive in the most glorious way. Your forgiveness is his *fact*, not your *feeling*. I know that's offensive to say in our "but how do you feel?" culture, but it's true. God's compassion doesn't need your consent. His pardon doesn't need your permission. His salvation doesn't need your stamp of approval. It just is. So, feelings, put that in your pipe and smoke it!

I studied all 128 uses of the words *forgive/forgiven/forgiveness* in the Bible. And how many of them were followed by the word *yourself*? Zero. I'll give you time to count to zero. Got it? Zero. Because God doesn't want to wait until we feel it or accept it or really agree with it. He just says it, declares it, proclaims it—you are forgiven. By the blood of Jesus Christ, you are forgiven.

Let me prove it: **"The blood of Jesus, his Son, purifies us from all sin"** (1 John 1:7). From all sin. You don't need to speak Greek to get that. All sin. Every sin. Your sin. Purified by the blood of Jesus. I may not know what it is, what you did, how bad it was, but God does. He knows even better than you, and yet look at what he promises. All sin. You are purified from all sin. He's done with it. He's forgiven it. His face isn't smiling upon you because he forgot about it. He knows, and he still has chosen to love you.

Or how about this? **"Therefore, there is now no condemnation for those who are in Christ Jesus"** (Romans 8:1). If you are "in Christ," if you trust that

Jesus died for you, there is now no condemnation. Consequences? Sure, lots of them. But condemnation, anger from God, distance from him. No. None of that. This verse comes right after the part where Paul says, "I do stuff I hate. I can't believe I keep doing that. What a wretched idiot I am." Paul feels what we feel, but he doesn't end with his feelings but with the fact of his forgiveness. In fact, in his original Greek, the verse says, "NONE, therefore, NOW (no) condemnation." None. God isn't even close to condemning you. That's true right now! Not years later, once time heals those wounds. No, right now you are forgiven. That's the fact.

Six years ago my now sixth grader was just a little kindergartner. But we had a conversation about forgiveness that stuck with me. I looked back at her car seat and asked, "Brooklyn, do you think Daddy is a good person?"

"No," she said (rather casually in my opinion).

"No. You think Daddy is a bad person?"

"Yes. Daddy sins."

"Oh, do you think God loves bad people?"

"Yes, Daddy," she said, as if it was obvious.

"But, sweetie, what if Daddy did something really bad? Really, really bad?"

"God would still love you, Daddy." And that was it. And she was right.

Friends, don't complicate it. What some of us sang back when we were kids is true today: "Jesus loves me; this I know, for the Bible tells me so." "Amazing grace, how sweet the sound, that saved a wretch like me." It's all still true. Even for you.

All of us face feelings that are just lies in disguise. But then we gather in church together, and we hear the truth from God. Then we do life with a group of people who love Jesus and then confront our false feelings. Then we grow in our faith with a podcast, and the Spirit reminds us of things that are so easy to forget. When we do these things, we produce fruit—not perfect fruit, but fruit like the peace and joy of knowing we are forgiven. Yes, even for that. Yes, even for all of it.

So let me finish this up with some help. First, I'd like you to go outside and find a stone. Think about that particular sin that is so hard for you to let go of. Now grab a Sharpie and draw a cross on that stone. Etch the ink into that stubborn rock. Let it be a reminder that Jesus died and rose for that sin too. I want you to keep that stone. It might be hard to forget the past, but you don't have to forget his promise—you are forgiven.

Then we can do what Jeremiah did. Check out these words:

**I remember my affliction and my wandering, the bitterness and the gall. I well remember them, and my soul is downcast within me. Yet this I call to mind and therefore I have hope:**

**Because of the Lᴏʀᴅ's great love we are not consumed, for his compassions never fail. They are new every morning; great is your faithfulness.** (Lamentations 3:19-23)

You and I remember what we did. But we refuse to forget what Jesus did. Great was his faithfulness. And that is why we are forgiven!

# *for further study*

# I CAN'T FORGIVE MYSELF

*Pastor Ben Sadler*

Throughout this book, we have looked at how we might forgive and heal when we have been sinned against. But what if we are the ones who have sinned? What if we cheated, relapsed, hurt, or wronged someone we love? How can we forgive ourselves, heal, and move on? Out of all the people whom God is calling you to forgive, forgiving yourself might be the most challenging. Let's look at the steps you can take to have mercy on your soul.

### Recognize your sin is worse than you thought

Pastor Mike says that refusing to forgive yourself is pure arrogance. He explains that our sin didn't just start with "that one big sin." As King David wrote, **"Surely I was sinful at birth, sinful from the time my mother conceived me"** (Psalm 51:5). In other words, we need God to forgive all our sins, which goes back to our earliest moments.

That same David also wrote about God's abundant forgiveness for ALL of our sins.

> **The Lᴏʀᴅ is compassionate and gracious,**
> **slow to anger, abounding in love.**
> **He will not always accuse,**

> nor will he harbor his anger forever;
> he does not treat us as our sins deserve
>   or repay us according to our iniquities.
> For as high as the heavens are above the earth,
>   so great is his love for those who fear him;
>  as far as the east is from the west,
>   so far has he removed our transgressions from us.
> (Psalm 103:8-12)

## Discuss or journal

Explain why it is important for us to see our sin as a much bigger problem than we originally thought.

_____

_____

_____

_____

_____

_____

_____

_____

_____

## Practice

Take a moment to write on a separate sheet of paper as many sins as you can remember. Not just the "big ones" but the less noticeable ones too. Then crumple up that piece of paper and throw it in the trash. (Burning it might be a good visual as well.)

## Recognize God's forgiveness is not based on your feelings

So much of the pain we suffer because of our sin is emotional pain. Guilt can feel like getting punched in the gut. Shame can feel like a crippling sadness. There might be moments when we feel the relief of forgiveness, but those feelings might be fleeting. We might argue with a pastor or friend who tells us we are forgiven.

But Jesus' life, death, and resurrection are historical facts. We can't change those facts. Two thousand years ago, Jesus lived as our substitute, died as a payment for our sin, and rose again to show his triumph over our deaths.

## Discuss or journal

List the range of feelings that you have experienced concerning your guilt. What do the highs and lows feel like? What happens to those feelings when you hear the facts about God's love and forgiveness for you?

## Confess your sins to one another
## so that you may be healed

Maybe one of the reasons you continue to struggle with guilt is because you are taking up this struggle all by yourself. Christianity was never meant to be an individual experience. We were called into a family of believers, into the body of Christ, into the community of faith. As long as you try to deal with your sins by yourself, the devil can continue to accuse you. Guilt is like mold. It grows in the darkness.

That's why James wrote, **"Therefore confess your sins to each other and pray for each other so that you may be healed"** (James 5:16). When we confess our sins out loud to each other, we break the chains of evil and get an opportunity to hear words of forgiveness.

### Discuss or journal

What keeps you from confessing your sins to others? How can you overcome those fears?

_____

_____

_____

_____

_____

## Practice

Consider calling a pastor or a friend and confessing the sin that you are struggling with. Also, consider asking a pastor to give you the Lord's Supper as a visual sign of God's personal forgiveness to you.

# About the Writers

**Pastor Mike Novotny** has served God's people in full-time ministry since 2007 in Madison and, most recently, at The CORE in Appleton, Wisconsin. He also serves as the lead speaker for Time of Grace, where he shares the good news about Jesus through television, print, and online platforms. Mike loves seeing people grasp the depth of God's amazing grace and unstoppable mercy. His wife continues to love him (despite plenty of reasons not to), and his two daughters open his eyes to the love of God for every Christian. When not talking about Jesus or dating his wife/girls, Mike loves playing soccer, running, and reading.

**Pastor Ben Sadler** has served as a full-time pastor since 2010. He began his ministry at a Spanish-speaking congregation in Florida. From 2014 to 2019, he served at Goodview Trinity Church in Minnesota. Currently, he is at Victory of the Lamb in Wisconsin. He is married to Emily, and they have three children. Ben loves to spend time with his family, ride his road bike, read, write, and preach.

# About Time of Grace

Time of Grace is an independent, donor-funded ministry that connects people to God's grace—his love, glory, and power—so they realize the temporary things of life don't satisfy. What brings satisfaction is knowing that because Jesus lived, died, and rose for all of us, we have access to the eternal God—right now and forever.

To discover more, please visit timeofgrace.org or call 800.661.3311.

# Help share God's message of grace!

Every gift you give helps Time of Grace reach people around the world with the good news of Jesus. Your generosity and prayer support take the gospel of grace to others through our ministry outreach and help them experience a satisfied life as they see God all around them.

**Give today at timeofgrace.org/give or by calling 800.661.3311.**

Thank you!